# Cries of happiness

Amanda Gray

BookLeaf
Publishing

This one is for you Grandma. I love you.

# These horrors should only belong in movies.

He said 'Concentration, camp.'

I thought I do love to camp, 'a camp with friends, beer and lots of food to eat', I said.

He shook his head and said, 'just listen'.

I thought, where's the music?

Rain slapped against the window

Bursts of white light came through the window, 'Blitzkrieg'.

'Blitzkrieg', he shouted, pointing his index finger to the sky, like puffs of smoke rolled across the sky.

I held his stiff hand and urged him to speak.

'Concentration camps. Don't run, or they will find you.'

Don't run, he thought every day, but he wanted to.

He's watched them clip off rounds, hosed them
down, once they escape, they can't try again.

He's seen horrors that should only belong in
movies.
'Concentration camps, stay long enough you
will watch others be set free.'

Herded them, my friends towards a black room,
I never saw them again
Set free, through the air,
apparitions lifted,
Higher than the gas chambers,
Flying free like birds.

Floated screams,
Groans,
Dead,
Dead silence.

He's heard horrors that should only belong in
movies.

Their eyes burned in the sun,

Sparkled like fool's gold,

Flies sucked away the spark of life,
Decay in the pit.

He lifts his head,

His body does not follow,

Blood drips down,

Shiny eyes,

Swallowed memories,

Lingered from unshed tears,

Leaking out like a prisoner.

Consumed by the eyes of its enemies,

Dry, dead, no more.

He's seen horrors that should only belong in
movies.

His face is worn out,
wrinkled as the old boots he once fought in,

His eyes were dirty brown,

Still stained with mud and blood.

His hands shake, he shakes to get the memory of
the innocents' blood

Off

Blood off,

Blood off,

His hands.

Droplets splatter,

      splatter across the mud,

            smoke clouds roll,

tumbling
      Over the sky.

Blood makes us who we are, it will control our
future.

He's done horrors that should only belong in
horror movies, but still, he did them.


Shadows passed across his faded eyes,

His grip fades,

In,

Out, and with his last breath.

He said, 'Don't make the same mistakes that I did'.

I nodded as my eyes filled with tears, I knew what he had done, and I will follow his advice even if it gets me killed.

I will only see the horrors he's seen in movies.

# Horizon

6

Sunrise shattered the dawn,

Songs floated like ghosts,

We meet the sun,

As our last,

Horizon.

# These hands

These hands,

Blood drips,

Blood drips off,

Blood off these hands,

These hands,

Are,

Not,

Mine!

# Together

8

Legs of satin,

We glide together,

Making sounds we shouldn't dare to make.

# I just can't

Ripped skin,

I chew my skin

Off my fingers,

My mind shakes,

Breathe,

Just breathe,

I just can't.

# Voices

They call my name,

I turn,

No one is there,

I turn back,

These Voices,

Haunt me.

# His lips

Drip drop,

Drip drop,

Past my lips,

Drip drop,

Blood drips,

It slips,

Down my hips,

Past my lips.

Lips to lips,

Flesh against flesh,

Heartache fuels me,

My lips taste him one last time.

# My poison

12

One-shot,

Is not enough,

Two shot,

No,

I need more,

Three shot,

Four and five,

The pain is gone,

But it will be back tomorrow.

# I will remember

Under the tree,

We waited for my bus,

I will remember,

You taught me how to be independent,

I will remember,

Your kisses covered my birthday cards and my face,

I will remember,

You listened to my imagination,

I will remember you.

# Farewell

14

Your mind passed away,

A year ago,

I stayed with you,

Until your mind disappeared,

Your words are a mess,

We can't understand,

You have become a shell.

# Goodbye

15

We sat,

On opposite sides of the bed,

Hand in hand,

We cried,

We talked,

We said goodbye,

We waited,

For a week,

Until your body passed.

# Free

You looked beautiful,

In your long sleep,

At peace,

Stone cold,

To the touch,

Frozen,

But Finally free.

# I know you

I knew you once,

Now,

I love a stranger,

I knew you once,

Now,

I cry for the past,

I knew you once,

Now,

You are lying to us,

To me,

I thought I knew you once.

# Timeline

18

We watch each other,

Obsessed,

What are they doing now?

We compare our life,

Obsessed,

We all have our own life,

Our own timeline.

# Words hurt

19

Words hurt,

With a poison tongue,

Words hurt,

And so do,

Sticks and stones.

# Bodies hit the floor

One,

Two,

Three,

Bodies hit the floor,

No warning,

They hit the floor,

Four,

Five,

Six,

Peachy keen on playing make-believe.

I followed my sisters' strides like stepping
stones of life.

Step,

Step,

Stumble,

Her feet would go on like a fairy tale.

Every mistake she'd make I would learn from
but instead,

I made my own mistakes in life.

Are we still peachy keen on playing
make-believe?

I am.

# I'm peachy keen on playing make-believe.

Endurance made me laugh at most of my life,

these scars run deep,

tattered,

but they still hold me together.

Steel caged heart for good measure but its
weakness,

fire.

Everything has a weakness.

Mine is trusting people!

Not anymore,

they need to earn my trust.

Earning trust is like money.

Is there anything else to keep me alive?

I'm too old to keep playing make-believe.

# Are you still peachy keen on playing make-believe?

Stop daydreaming,

they shouted,

and grow up,

Are you still peachy keen on playing
make-believe?

Teen angst,

defied,

crazy with instinct,

Are you still peachy keen on playing
make-believe?

As adults,

we think we know what we are doing,

but we pretend,

until we realize we are just kids with houses,

Are you still peachy keen on playing
make-believe?

# consequences

We can never escape the consequence,
we can only survive them.

Overdosing is not fun, waking up in hospital
with the police waiting on either side of the
door.

Kidneys dying,

Wake up in hospital with your family
surrounding you,

they wanted to help you but you didn't listen.

Beep, beep, beep.

They don't know how to help you anymore.

Scars appear on your skin as well as inside your
mind,

They will never fully heal, leaving rips in the
skin like craters,

a reminder that you survived the consequences.

# Time

27

We watch the clock,

but we don't keep the time.